Nurturing Environment Model
Handbook

AMIR LEVINE, PH.D., LCSW-R

BHAVA
Therapy Group

ISBN paperback: 9798690417413

Printed in USA

Visit our website at www.bhavatherapygroup.com

INTRODUCTION

Welcome! My name is Dr. Amir Levine, and I am the co-founder and Clinical Director of Bhava Therapy Group. During my 20 years of practicing psychotherapy, I have had the true pleasure and honor of working with a growing population of older adults (ages 60+). I have found working with this cohort to be extremely rewarding, challenging, and meaningful, on a deep and profound level. It is amazing to me that older adults have struggled with certain stereotypes in the past that labeled them as inappropriate for psychotherapy and not compatible with its goals; nothing can be further from the truth and, on the contrary, I find that older adults have the knowledge, temperament, and readiness to make more use of therapy than any other age population.

Additionally, older adults bring with them a force of focus, urgency, and maturity interwoven in a profound period in their lives that finds them seeking to make sense of a full life lived while searching for safety and clarity for their futures. Their existential readiness to delve into questions of mortality, purpose, and meaning is nurtured by the growing awareness of their physical fragility and the losses they have experienced. In my work with older adults I have discovered an eagerness to enjoy life and a motivation and willingness to work on enhancing their mental health and sense of joy. I believe that there is a similarity and parallel between a child's search for self and identity and the older adult's pursuit of meaning, purpose, and self-acceptance in his/her life. However, older adulthood brings with it the question of identity and another layer of complexity. Whereas children may ask, "Who am I becoming and who am I yet to be?," older adults are asking, "Who have I been?" and, based on that, "Who will I continue to be?" During both childhood and older adulthood, there are profound windows of opportunity through which we as clinicians can impact the trajectories of our patients' lives. However, with older adults, this extraordinarily important period in identity formation is more complex, and is situated right at the pinnacle of their coming to terms with the past, and their planning for the future. This makes our connections with older adults ever more important, and it demands unique skill sets.

The psychoanalyst Donald Winnicott discussed the importance of creating a *holding environment* for children in the psychotherapy process, in which they feel seen, accepted, and supported, and where their true selves can emerge. I believe that clinicians working with older adults should strive to create a *nurturing environment*, where their need for exploration, safety, and connection can flourish and where their need for acceptance can emerge. To this end, I will present a model of practice called the **Nurturing Environment Model (NEM).** As I said before, there is a striking parallel between the emergence of self during childhood and the experiences of older age; both phases of life are rich with opportunities for awareness and growth.

This first segment of the book begins by discussing the mental health needs of older adults, along with important statistical data. I then shift to the evolution of psychotherapeutic care with older adults, from the inception of psychotherapy to the present day.

The next chapter examines aspects of normative aging. In order for clinicians to be effective, helpful, and unbiased toward older adults, it is imperative that we understand the social, psychological, and emotional aspects of normative aging and the normal aspects of emotional and psychological development for this age group. Chapter Four transitions to the client-clinician relationship. The most important element of any therapeutic model is the client-clinician relationship, and this chapter will focus on how to enhance the unique and essential elements of this relationship when it comes to older adults. Chapter Five introduces and describes the NEM model. I find that the clinical needs of older adults can be complex and multidimensional. As such, it is my clinical opinion that in order for us to be effective clinicians we would benefit from a model and approach to care that is expansive in scope and which uses the best of many modalities of care. NEM is an eclectic therapeutic approach that is informed by and incorporates knowledge from various modalities and schools of thought, including cognitive behavioral, sensorimotor psychotherapy, positive psychology, postmodern psychology, systems theory, and psychodynamic modalities. The final segment of this handbook addresses behavioral assessment and management of dementia, a condition that is prevalent among the older adult population and will most likely continue to grow in prevalence as people live longer. Dementia affects not just the individual, but the entire family caring for him or her; it is essential that clinicians know the basics of how to properly identify, assess, support, and manage clients diagnosed with dementia.

My hope is that this handbook will be helpful in guiding you in your work with older adult clients, and will help clinicians and clients feel supported and nurtured.

TABLE OF CONTENTS

UNDERSTANDING THE NEED

Some of us are surprised to learn about the mental health needs of older adults and are not aware of our own biases in the way we view this population. Due to older people's growing physical fragility, we tend to focus our attention on the physical aspects of their care while neglecting their emotional, psychological, and social needs.

It is vital that, as clinicians, we become aware of the importance of the mental health needs and overall wellbeing of older adults so that we can treat, educate, and advocate for their psychosocial care, incorporating their mental, social, and physical treatment in our support.

Statistical data shed light on the importance of focusing on the mental health needs of older adults.

According to the December 2017 report, World Health Organization on Mental Health of Older Adults; data from the 2018 *Alzheimer's Disease Facts and Figures*; and the American Psychological Association:

- Over 20 percent of adults aged 60 and above suffer from a mental or neurological disorder. The most common of these are depression and dementia.

- As many as 20 percent of older adults and up to 37 percent of nursing home residents suffer from depression.

- About 70 percent of all primary care visits are driven by psychological factors (i.e. stress, depression), which points to the fact that medical, psychological, emotional, and social factors are inextricably linked. Many older adults will initially report their symptoms as physical, but through further inquiry we can find the psychological, emotional, and/or social issues that may enhance or trigger medical complaints and visits.

- While older adults make up 13 percent of the population, they account for 25 percent of the people who commit suicide, making depression more likely to be lethal for this group. Therefore, it is essential that clinicians and medical providers assess for depression with older adults. Family members should also be encouraged to identify symptoms of depression and encourage those afflicted to reach out for support. [A validated and useful depression screening tool for older adults is the *Geriatric Depression Scale*, which can be found in the appendix of this handbook.]

- It is staggering that one in six adults over the age of 60 has experienced some form of abuse and exploitation during the past year. It is vital that clinicians assess for safety with all older adults and inquire about relationships and commitments that may be suspicious and exploitative in nature. [A validated and helpful abuse screening tool is the *Elder Abuse Screening*

Index (EASI), which is located in the appendix of this handbook.]

- A statistic that may be surprising for some is that substance abuse is one of the eight leading causes of death for older people, and it is estimated that 17 percent of this group misuses and abuses alcohol and medications. Therefore, it is as important to inquire and assess for substance abuse with older adults as it is with any other client population, and ensure the proper use of their prescribed medications. [A validated and helpful screening tool that clinicians can use to assess for alcohol abuse is the *Short Michigan Alcohol Screening Test—Geriatric Version* (SMAST-G), which you can find in the appendix of this handbook.]

- It is estimated that one in six women and one in ten men will develop dementia during their lifetimes.

- One in three seniors dies from complications associated with dementia, and it kills more people than breast and prostate cancer combined. Initial screenings are important for the best outcome. [A validated and helpful abuse screening is the Washington University Dementia Screening Test, which is located in the appendix of this handbook.]

- Thirty percent of people over the age of 85 are afflicted with dementia. Often times with dementia comes a wide range of psychiatric symptoms, such as paranoid ideations, psychotic features, aggression, and depression, placing a great toll on clients and their caregivers. As such, there is a great need for mental health services among this population.

It is important that clinicians focus on monitoring and assessing older adults' mental health, substance abuse, vulnerability to exploitation/victimization, and risk for dementia. As we will discuss, older people's vulnerability is three-fold:

First, they present with an interconnected range of psychological, emotional, social, and health-related issues that initially may masquerade as physical symptoms.

Second, due to social biases, older adults tend to be overlooked and ignored as a population when it comes to assessment and management of psychosocial aspects of care. Clinicians working with older adults need to be aware of societal biases and their own prejudices when it comes to this population. Awareness of biases can greatly enhance our ability to work them through and enhance our effectiveness as clinicians and agents of change.

Third, older adults have to grapple with their own biases and stigmas about mental health, seeking help, and psychotherapy. Some in this group grew up in times where psychotherapy was for "crazy people" and depression was considered a moral weakness. As we will discuss in later chapters, clinicians working with older adults can work toward de-stigmatizing and educating clients on the benefits of psychotherapy.

I hope that those reading this book who treat older adults will make sure to conduct a thorough and thoughtful assessment of their clients.

THE EVOLUTION OF ATTITUDES

The approach and perception of psychotherapy with older adults has evolved significantly.

Sigmund Freud is quoted as saying in the early 1900s, "Near or above the age of fifty the elasticity of the mental processes, on which the treatment depends, is as a rule lacking," pointing to the sentiment at that time that older adults lack the cognitive ability to participate in psychotherapy and, in a sense, have missed the boat on psychotherapy and are too late to be helped. Of course, this view of older adults as being incompatible with the process of psychotherapy resulted in a sense of hopelessness among clients, clinicians, and caregivers when it came to treatment.

The failure to recognize later adulthood as a clinically significant development phase can be seen in the dearth of psychoanalytic theory and writing about middle and later life, in contrast to the attention paid to infancy and childhood.

This discriminatory approach—or neglect altogether—when it comes to psychotherapy, coincides with the broader phenomenon of ageism, which is defined as the stereotyping and discrimination of individuals based on their age. The recent recognition of ageism as a phenomenon has helped shed light and create an awareness of the ways in which society views older age as a less valued and less useful stage in life, resulting in emotional isolation and even neglect of the elderly. Some theories hold that embedded in the aversion to older age may be a psychological fear of death of the younger majority who, when interacting with older adults, are reminded of their own mortality.

The Swiss psychiatrist and psychoanalyst Carl Jung (1933) was the first psychodynamic theorist to identify positive and enhancing traits of old age that may actually provide older adults with certain advantages compared to younger psychotherapy clients. Jung viewed later adulthood as a time of wisdom, inner exploration, and introspection, a way to find meaning and wholeness that makes life acceptable. This was an important paradigm shift that not only conveyed the message that older adults can engage in psychotherapy, but that they also have a unique set of developmental attributes that can make psychotherapy especially growth-promoting, compared to any other client population.

The German-American developmental psychologist Erik Erikson (1951) created a lifespan developmental task perspective comprising eight stages. Erikson's pioneering work was significant because it expressed the belief that human development continues throughout the entire lifespan and does not end at 6 years old as traditional psychoanalytic theorists believed. We are continuously evolving and becoming during our entire lifespan. In each stage of Erikson's model, there is a developmental task that needs to be achieved, and a possible negative outcome if the task is not accomplished. Of particular interest to our discussion is the last and crucial stage in Erikson's lifespan model: *ego integrity vs. ego despair*, which occurs in late adulthood.

In later adulthood, one can have a positive outcome by reaching ego integrity through developing a sense of acceptance of oneself and the life that one has lived. So, an individual may say, "My life and I may not have been perfect, but I still love myself and the life that I have lived." A person who has reached ego integrity will be able to find meaning and a sense of purpose, viewing his/her life as a life that needed to be lived as is, whether it was finding meaning in raising children, reaching vocational aspirations, or overcoming challenges. According to Erikson, we can also find in the ego integrity stage an acceptance and readiness for death, which comes from feeling whole and complete, and a tenderness and love of humanity. When ego integrity is not achieved, and ego despair takes over, this can result in enhanced fear of death and difficulty accepting one's life. Possible regret, sadness, and feelings of anger may ensue.

Pearl King (1974) drew attention to the life stage factors that contribute to the openness of older adults to engage in therapy. Some examples of these are the feeling that this is the last chance to bring change or a new understanding to their lives, and the immediacy of actual losses that make it more difficult to deny anxiety about life transition and change. As such, exposure to illness, fragility, and death may heighten the urgency to grapple with questions and fears about mortality and change, providing new opportunities to address very important issues in therapy (Gorsuch, 1998).

According to an article written in *The New York Times* by Abby Ellen in 2013, an increasing number of older adults are seeking psychotherapy more than ever before. There is greater recognition of the need for mental health services, while at the same time the negative stigma of it has been lifted. There is also a greater recognition among clinicians that older adults make great psychotherapy clients, as they tend to be more motivated and focused on their goals. They also tend to understand the importance of utilizing their time effectively.

So now that we can understand how older adult clients can benefit from psychotherapy as much as, if not even more so, than other populations, let's look at how we can understand what aging actually means.

According to "The Lifecourse Perspective on Aging: Linked Lives, Timing and History" (Bengtson & Allen, 1993), aging is a biological and sociocultural process. We all have a biological and social clock that work together. We all have an evident biological process of aging. Our bodies change while our skin texture and body mass shift. But there are also social changes and expectations that may accompany the process of aging, such as assuming the role of a grandparent, becoming a retiree, and transitioning out of one's working productive years. We expect older adults to have more time on their hands. It is also expected that older adults be gentler, kinder, and wiser.

It is also important to note that aging is a socially relative process and may be experienced differently, depending on one's culture, time, and geographical location. For instance, in modern Western cultures, we are heavily influenced by the Protestant work ethic which promotes productivity, the ability to care for oneself, and success. In this context, aging is often experienced unfavorably because it is associated with loss of value. Additionally, modern society's emphasis on youth, beauty, and individuality may further serve to alienate older adults who then question their sense of inherent value.

Erikson summarized it well when he wrote that we are "lacking a cultural viable ideal for old age, our civilization does not really harbor a concept of the whole life" (Erikson, 1997, page 114). As such, we can see that as a society we have a narrow scope of the beauty and the opportunities that are embedded in the aging process. Our perception and understanding of older adulthood, like many other developmental phases and tasks, are socially constructed. This means that society has provided us with a set of expectations, ideals, and values that we have internalized either consciously or subconsciously. As we discussed earlier, in Western cultures, older adults often feel less valued, marginalized, and invisible as they struggle with ageism.

In an article by the Huffington Post (2014) we can see examples from other cultures where older adulthood is perceived within a lens of celebration and value.

- *In Greece*, elders are honored and celebrated. Respect for older people is a fundamental component of family life. Abbots in Greece, who head monasteries, are addressed by everyone as "Gerondas," meaning "elder man." It can be inferred that older people have a sacred and highly respected status.

- *Native American* culture recognizes elders' key role in passing down their knowledge to younger family members; their role as educators and shapers of the younger generation is of great importance.

- *In Korea,* aging is rooted in the principle of filial piety, a value dictating respect for one's parents. All are socialized to revere older individuals. The "Hwangap" 60th birthday celebrates accomplishment, and the 70th birthday "Gohui" marks the celebrant as old and rare. Both are big, momentous celebrations to celebrate the social significance of older age.

- **Many *East Indians*** live in multi-generational families with the elders holding the key role as head of the household and advisor on various financial and interpersonal issues. Due to its emphasis on the values of connectedness, duty, respect, and acceptance of death as a natural part of the lifecycle, East Indian society greatly respects and values older adulthood (Sushi, 2016).

In the aforementioned examples we can see the significance of societal value systems and social perception in determining whether or not older adulthood is viewed with respect, hope, and celebration. As clinicians, it is vital that we serve as educators and advocates for clients, families, health workers, and society at large, to uphold the profound opportunities that are embedded in older age as well as celebrate the unique skills, abilities, and strengths that older adult clients often possess.

ASPECTS OF NORMATIVE AGING

As with any developmental phase, the process of aging will include age-appropriate psychological, behavioral, and physical changes. The reason it is important to discuss the normative aspects of aging is because too often we associate it with pathology. The following are normative aging developments that occur in older adults that may often be distorted and viewed as a pathology, contributing to a culture that is non-accepting, judging, demanding, and non-nurturing to older adults:

1. ***Focusing attention inward***: Increased focus on inner life and decreased attachment to people, demands, expectations, and objects in the outer world. This often is accompanied by a reduced appetite for power and ambition. We may encounter older adults who are more inwardly focused and less reactive to external stimuli. Knowing this is vital in helping us distinguish depression from the normative aspects of going inward in an older adult.

2. ***Fluid intelligence***: This is defined as the ability to identify patterns, solve problems, and think abstractly, which may be reduced in older adults. Crystalized intelligence, which is defined as the ability to use and retrieve learned knowledge and experience, remains stable. Too often we pathologize the natural process of shifting fluid intelligence during later adulthood,

creating unnecessary alarm and a sense of doubt and inadequacy for older adults (Woods,1999).

3. ***Re-evaluation of the past***: During older adulthood there may be a growing tendency and need to look back on one's life in an ongoing process of acceptance and coming to terms. At times, one's past decisions and life choices may be questioned and processed. Although the process of looking back and questioning may at times appear to the outsider as a symptom of depression, especially when it is accompanied by a sense of regret and doubt, it may be part of a necessary process of reaching a certain level of acceptance.

4. ***Heightened awareness of mortality and time***: Older adults may tend to see things in terms of time left to live rather than time lived since birth, and with that comes an increased awareness that one's time is finite. This is a natural process of understanding one's mortality and concern about when and how life will come to its conclusion. Some family members, friends, and even clinicians can struggle with providing emotional support regarding mortality, and view it as a pessimistic personality attribute. They might thus respond to it with dismissiveness, avoidance, and attempts to overly reassure, resulting in the client feeling isolated, not listened to, and shameful about his/her natural developmental process.

5. ***Diminished emotional reactivity***: In older age there may be a slowing down of emotional reactivity. This

could be because the client has lived through a wide range of emotional experiences and is less surprised by new ones. Nevertheless, this shift should not be associated with depression or a negative change in mood; in fact this decreased reactivity can actually enhance the ability to make informed and less-impulsive decisions.

6. ***Fluidity in gender expectations***: Later adulthood may also bring changes to perceived gender roles and experiences of self. Men, for instance, may become more tolerant of their nurturing and affiliative impulses, and less concerned with power, while older women grow more accepting of their assertive impulses.

7. ***Increased preoccupation with physical health***: The impact of aging on physical performance and overall health is naturally a central concern of the elderly. As such, we may see more of an emphasis, focus, and expression of concern about their health and various physical symptoms. It is necessary for clinicians and family members supporting older adults to be able to understand, validate, and support this need to discuss and address health concerns (Lewis and Johansen, 1982).

8. ***Life happiness***: Studies have shown that happiness follows a U-shaped curve pattern with peaks of happiness at age 23, and then again at age 69 (Sutin, 2013). A happiness peak at the age of 69 may be surprising to many, but actually, if we ask older adults about their state of satisfaction in comparison to other stages of

life, we often find increased satisfaction and a sense of acceptance, less pressure to achieve and compete, with greater ability to be present and slow things down. As such, older adult clients may bring to the psychotherapy process and relationships in general a sense of joy and optimism that others can grow and learn from.

9. Finally, older people are believed to show better competencies for reasoning about social dilemmas and conflicts. They're more capable of seeing things from various points of view and of compromising, while being less emotionally reactive. There is something to the statement that with age comes wisdom. Older people may be able to bring to the psychotherapy process a certain readiness to learn and grow from social situations that may be missing at other developmental stages.

Psychotherapeutic themes: In working with older adults, it is important to be aware of certain psychotherapeutic themes or issues that may arise in treatment that are stage appropriate. Knowing these issues—they are listed below—and being prepared to address them head-on, is important in our work with older adults:

1. *Invisibility*: Older adults may feel increasingly "left out," "irrelevant," and some report a sense of "not being seen." The attention and recognition they received as younger adults is not the same. The aforementioned feelings are often related to the overall sense that with later adulthood comes a loss of professional, physical, and social status appeal, all contributing to a feeling of invisibility.

2. ***Loss:*** This is another major theme that often comes up in my work with older adults. As we age, we are more likely to experience various forms of loss, whether it be our health, loved ones, physical ability, or professional status. In sessions, clients may focus on one of these losses, or all of them.

3. ***Regret of life choices/decisions and unrealized dreams*** are other issues that can arise in treatment. Some clients will reflect back and deride themselves for certain choices and decisions that they did or did not make. For instance, some may conclude that they did not spend enough time with their children, while others regret not making certain vocational choices. As such, regret and guilt can be experienced as a result of either action or inaction, and can wreak emotional havoc.

4. ***Loneliness and social isolation*** are major issues discussed in the treatment of older adults. Almost half of women aged 75 and above live alone. By the time people reach age 85, fully 40 percent live by themselves. Social isolation has been linked to health problems, including dementia, heart disease, increased risk of hospital admission, and a heightened danger of falls. Loneliness has also been associated with weakened immune systems and cancer, and has been described as a "fertilizer" for diseases. Over a third of people over the age of 45 report feeling lonely. It is important to identify those clients and help link them to social support (National Institute on Aging, 2019).

5. ***Fear*** of the process of aging and physical decline, and the prospect of going through it alone, is another major concern of older adults, especially for those who live alone and lack support networks. Some clients have difficulty acknowledging that what they are experiencing is fear and worry about aging and the process of life coming to an end. Allowing clients to verbalize their fears may greatly enhance the feeling that they are not alone with their fears.

6. ***Chronic illness***: About 80 percent of older adults have a chronic illness that can result in disability. Some clients might be significantly impacted by their physical symptoms, and this may cause them great distress and hamper their ability to be active. Some older adults can underestimate their health issues and neglect themselves. For many, their health and physical concerns are a major part of their daily focus. Medical appointments, procedures, and bowel movements can all be part of the routine discussion. As such, they might have a need to discuss in great detail aspects of their illness and it is fundamental that clinicians working with this age group provide a nurturing environment for these vulnerable thoughts to be processed openly and freely in an accepting, non-judgmental, and warm therapeutic relationship.

THE CLIENT-THERAPIST RELATIONSHIP

The client relationship: As with all clients, the therapeutic relationship we cultivate with older adults is the key to any successful psychotherapeutic process. In my practice, I have found specific skills that can be utilized in our work with older clients that may greatly enhance the therapeutic relationship with them:

1. ***Psycho-education***: Many older clients born in an era when psychotherapy was not common may have misinformation or a lack of awareness of its process. As discussed earlier, some may view psychotherapy as "only for crazy people." As such, one of the first things I like to do with older adult clients is inform them on what therapy is and how it can help them. Older age may bring with it a certain set of habitual behaviors used as coping methods to manage stress. The process of psychotherapy is to ask people to experiment with new thoughts and behaviors and have a different dialogue with themselves. As such, it is important to ease the client into the process of psychotherapy by explaining it in layperson terms. For example, you might say, "Psychotherapy is a process that may help you feel more connected to yourself, develop self-awareness and can help you learn to manage stress and create meaningful change in your life. Sometimes psychotherapy may feel uncomfortable because you may be challenged to think and do things you haven't done before."

2. ***Home visits***: These are a wonderful way to develop trust and learn about clients in their home environments. Pictures, apartment settings, and furniture can help us learn so much about a patient's culture and history that words often can't convey. I also find that clients tend to feel more comfortable with their clinicians after they have let them into their own homes. It's almost as if they are saying, "You have seen me for who I am; now we can begin our work together."

3. ***Meeting the clients where they are***: Older clients may have developed lifestyles and routines that are comfortable and familiar to them, and that provide a sense of safety and control. At times, clinicians or family members with good intentions may want to advise and suggest changes to the client's lifestyle, habits, and routines (diet, sleep routines, exercise, for instance). However, clients can feel sensitive to suggestions that they view as impositions that infringe upon their lifestyles, habits, and ways of being in the world. It is most effective to meet clients where they are. It is essential to provide them with a sense of safety and control in the process. How can we do this? I usually begin the treatment process by informing clients that our sessions are centered around them and are for whatever they want to talk about. I want clients, especially older ones, to know that we are not trying to take over their lives, but rather to be there for them on the issues that they would like and are ready to address. Even though clients and I may know that it would benefit them to change certain behaviors, I still always check with

them that they are ready to address those behaviors. Rushing to change behaviors that they are not ready to address may scare them away and jeopardize the relationship. I find when offering suggestions, advice, and guidance, asking for permission to offer—in a sense "knocking on the door"—is very helpful, providing the client with a sense of control and autonomy. I find that asking that simple question can facilitate an openness to my feedback.

4. ***Begin with small wins***: When focusing on changing or modifying behavior, it is important to begin with small wins and achievable tasks. Before embarking on behavioral change, there should be mutual agreement with the client expressing willingness and some level of initial ability to succeed at the task. For example, an elderly client struggling with morbid obesity initially declined to join an exercise class which he felt would be "too much for me," but agreed to walk down his building hallway for ten minutes two times a week. This was an achievable task that provided the impetus for more challenging behavior changes in his lifestyle and diet.

5. ***Tailoring sessions to physical limitations***: It is important that sessions be tailored to the needs of the client and move at a slower pace in order to accommodate cognitive and sensory changes that come with later adulthood, along with other medical conditions such as difficulty with hearing, vision, and the processing of information. I always check with the client that I am not talking too softly or quickly; I am often asked

to speak louder, more clearly, and more slowly. It is important to make clients who are sensitive to light or noise comfortable. Likewise for those who are struggling with general body and back pain — make sure that they are comfortable in their seats. Again, the key is checking in with the client and making special accommodations accordingly.

6. ***Collaborate with support networks***: Because many older adults may rely on their support networks, a great way to learn about them is to interview those in these networks including friends and family. Extremely beneficial information can be gained through such questions as, "What can you tell me about the client that would be important for me to know?" or, "From your experience, what support do you think would benefit the client?" Collaborating with clients' support networks can be highly effective in providing the consistent, effective, and optimal care that they need. For example, clients who are forgetful about their appointments and medications can be supported by friendly reminders from their support networks.

7. ***It is particularly important to contact, meet with, and solicit help*** from support networks when it comes to older adults who are increasingly vulnerable due to dementia and other debilitating medical conditions; it is helpful to enlist them as co-supporters in the care of the client. However, it is vital that any discussion with the family involves the patient's consent. In situations where the client has agreed for a proxy to make deci-

sions for him/her, it is important to regularly involve and update that proxy about the client's continued care as well as his/her thoughts, feelings, and decisions that have arisen in psychotherapy.

8. ***Checking-in on special occasions:*** As mentioned earlier, older adults may have fewer social interactions and can experience loneliness and feelings of invisibility. Birthdays, various anniversaries such as that of the passing of a loved one, and holidays can intensify the feeling of loneliness. Brief phone calls and/or texts to check in can be highly important to help them feel cared-for, and ease their loneliness and isolation.

9. ***Validation, empathic stances, and reflection skills:*** These are important relationship-building skills and are the most important ingredients for treatment, especially with older adults, who are usually much more attuned to the manner of and connection with the therapist. A validating statement such as, "It makes sense that you feel that you're living in fear since the fall," acknowledges the thoughts and feelings of a client. Empathy goes deeper in reflecting the emotional experience of the client by, for example, telling them, "It must feel scary since the fall, and seems that it can happen again any minute." Using both validating and empathic skills can be powerful in treatment. Helping the client feel understood and not alone in her/his experience is the key factor in creating the nurturing environment for treatment.

10. ***Educating ourselves:*** Working with older adults from different cultural milieus or who have been exposed to historical events unfamiliar to their clinician will require that the latter educate themselves on these historical and cultural influences that have impacted and shaped clients throughout their lives. This can involve researching famous singers, writers, actors, and historical events that have left an impact on the client. Reading books and articles, and seeing movies are also great ways to learn about and get the feel of the social context of clients' lives. This information can provide you with a point of reference and more in-depth context to connect with, and view, the client.

11. ***Authentic use of self and appropriate self-disclosure:*** This can humanize the relationship and create a sense of warmth and emotional connection. Being ourselves and being comfortable with our spontaneous reactions as they arise in treatment is important. Older clients have been exposed to many social interactions in the past and may be very attuned to clinicians who are not comfortable in their own skin. When appropriate and beneficial, I find that self-disclosure can be a way to enhance trust and provide a point of access to discuss issues, circumstances, and relationships that could be of benefit to the client. For instance, when discussing a grief reaction with one of my clients, I shared with him that, "When I lost a grandfather with whom I was very close, I felt a great deal of regret and guilt that I had not spent more time with him before he passed."

Again, your most important therapeutic instrument is your *relationship*. Skills and knowledge are important, but if I were to put an emphasis on one specific aspect of treatment, it is your relationship with the client and your authentic presence strengthens that relationship. What clients seek most are positive authentic connections and nurturing therapeutic relationships.

THE NURTURING ENVIRONMENT MODEL (NEM)

It is my clinical judgment that a psychotherapeutic model for older adults is most effective when it addresses their past, present, and future in the context of their social, psychological, emotional, and biomedical needs. Similar to Winnicott's holding environment model, the nurturing environment model's goal is to create a holding environment for older adults with the focus on nurturing their strengths and needs through the use of interventions from various schools of thought. This eclectic model encompasses various interventions that have been shown to be effective with older adults.

The nurturing environment model includes five elements: Transference and countertransference; managing loss; life review; positive aging; and managing chronic illness.

As mentioned earlier, NEM is eclectic in nature, incorporating psychodynamics, behavioral activation, cognitive behavioral techniques, sensorimotor psychotherapy, positive psychology, psychodynamic, postmodern psychology, and systems theory. The model provides the client with the experience of being seen, valued, and accepted.

Through the use of transference and countertransference, the model focuses on helping the client manage interpersonal struggles and establish closer and more-meaningful relationships with his/her support networks. The model also strives to help clients process, accept, and grow from loss. NEM focuses on helping them establish coherent, accepting, and fulfilling stories about their lives with the use of the life review process. The model places an emphasis on nurturing patients' strengths that are already in place. NEM also strives to develop healthy coping skills to manage chronic illness and growing awareness of how emotions may be held in the body. NEM provides a place to explore and discuss patients' innermost fears, including death, disability, loneliness, guilt, and regret, all within a safe, warm, and nurturing environment.

NEM—Transference and Countertransference: The first element of the nurturing model is the management of transference and countertransference, a concept taken from psychodynamic theory. One of the intervention skills in working with older adults is knowing how to *recognize* and *utilize* the transference and countertransference that can arise in treatment. Transference is often understood to be a situation where the feelings, desires, and expectations of one person are redirected and applied to another, in this case the therapist. Countertransference is where the client evokes various feelings, thoughts, reactions, and memories in the clinician (Knight, 1996). I would like to discuss various types of transference and countertransference that can occur specifically in sessions with older adults. This has been well documented in literature focusing on psychodynamic work with older adults (Yesavage & Karasu, 1982; Kennedy & Tanenbaum, 2000).

Transference

Child transference is where older clients transfer parental feelings and attitudes toward the clinician. It may be experienced in issues relating to control where the client makes it a point to be in charge as a parental figure. For instance a client of mine expressed his discomfort with sharing his feelings with me regarding the loss of his wife because, "You are as old as my son and I would not share with him these feelings." Child transference may also manifest as the client appearing to lecture, guide, protect, and teach the clinician on different issues as they might do with their own children, toward whom they may want to impart their wisdom and care. Additionally, child transference may arise in the context of dependency, motivated by the care clients are receiving, or wish to receive, from their own children. So child transference may take the form of a client wishing to take control and assume power in the manner of a parent, as in "Respect me and do as I say," or it can happen with the expression of his/her need for dependency, as in "Help and take care of me as you would your parent." Transference may also play out in issues regarding trust where clients find it difficult or easy to trust, depending on their relationship with their own children.

Parental transference is different, and occurs when the client transfers his/her need to be parented onto the clinician. In this situation, the clinician will likely feel a parental responsibility for the client. A good example of this is when the client asks the clinician to call every day to offer reassurance, resulting in the clinician feeling overwhelmed. This type of transference is most likely to occur with clients in a regressed state and with a high degree of dependency as a result of trauma.

Grandchild transference is when the client transfers the feelings and expectations of a grandparent onto the clinician. This is often a more positive and warmer type of transference, as grandparents tend to cherish the relationship with their grandchildren, and it is one that is often less conflicted. Oftentimes, the clinician may feel in this situation that the client is idealizing him or her. The clinician may be able to utilize this positive transference to help the client through behavioral change. For instance, a client of mine agreed to listen to my advice of checking his insulin daily because I was "sweet" like his grandchild and he didn't want to "disappoint" me.

Erotic transference is where sexual feelings toward the clinician develop. Older adults' erotic transference may at times be overlooked, denied, or minimized. However, it is common for the client's need for intimacy and dependency to lead to erotic feelings and fantasies toward the clinician. This can arise, for example, with a client asking personal questions about the status or history of the clinician's intimate relationships. In a situation like this it is important that the clinician educates the client about the boundaries of the therapeutic relationship, explaining that he/she will not answer personal questions that are not related to the therapeutic relationship.

Authority transference can have clients playing out their own relationships with authority figures in their lives, and can evoke a wide range of feelings and reactions in the client. The clinician in this situation may observe the client treating him/her with great importance, or showing fear and dependency; alternatively the client may react with hostility, resistance, detachment, and anger. Sometimes a client might experience all the aforementioned feelings.

The major goal with all transference processes is for the clinician to allow himself/herself to be a vehicle through which clients can gain awareness of how they experience themselves in relationships. It is hoped that through this awareness, patients' relationships can be enhanced in meaningful ways.

Countertransference

Here are some common countertransference feelings that the clinician may experience in working with older adults:

Authority figure issues can arise as a common countertransference reaction when working with older adults, in which the clinician views the client as an authority figure. Through a sense of fear or respect, clinicians may feel a reluctance to question their clients' decisions or provide feedback. For instance, a clinician working with a client who reminds him of his feared father may struggle with setting limits and boundaries with a client who at times may be disrespectful during sessions.

Fear of death and illness is another common countertransference reaction that may arise in working with older adults. The tendency to associate older age with illness and the end of life may bring up clinicians' own fears and ambivalence about death and illness. This is an extremely powerful countertransference that can make it challenging for certain clinicians to work with older adults, causing them to be overcome with their own pain and fears, and leaving them emotionally depleted and powerless to care for their clients. It is vital that clinicians struggling with countertransference issues with death and illness get help in processing and managing their own experience with loss and grief.

Fear of powerlessness may occur when discussing such highly charged topics as illness, the end of life, and life's regrets. These discussions may provoke feelings in the clinician of helplessness, fear, inadequacy, and professional incompetence. These feelings may be picked up from the client's own feelings of doubt, fear, and powerlessness.

Parental countertransference is a common reaction experienced by clinicians when a client reminds them of a father or mother. Depending on the clinician's relationship with his/her parents, these feelings may involve warmth, distance, ambivalence, guardedness, or resentment. For instance, a colleague experienced strong negative reactions toward an 85-year-old client with a history of alcohol dependence and who had been out of contact with his three children. This was triggered by my colleague's strong negative feelings and associations toward his own father. When parental countertransference arises that may negatively impact the therapeutic process, it is vital for clinicians to seek support for their own unresolved processes. This will help them both process these painful issues and better support their clients.

Positive countertransference is where the client experiences positive, warm, and trusting feelings toward the client. The risk here is that too much warmth will blur the therapeutic boundaries and impair the therapist's ability to be effective and objective (Nordhus & Nielsen, 1999). In one scenario a clinician sensing his client's dependency decided to make a daily house call, feeding him and making financial decisions on his behalf. This assumption of control over the patient's daily life resulted in a tense relationship with the patient's family who felt threatened by a perception that the clinician was "taking over."

The key issue with all countertransference is for the clinician to become aware of his/her emotional reactions toward the client and the associations, thoughts, and fantasies that the client may evoke. It is important for the clinician to be aware of all countertransference issues so that (1) they don't negatively impact the therapeutic process, and (2) they, along with the client's transference issues and projections, can be fully explored and processed for the benefit of the client.

Take the previous example of the clinician who experienced a positive countertransference to his client and ended up assuming control of the latter's daily life, **and in so doing responded and was reactive** to his transference for dependency and need to be taken care of. When the clinician's countertransference and client transference are brought into session, this can be a wonderful opportunity to discuss the latter's fantasy and, at times, legitimate need to be taken care of and assess the ways in which we can support the client without taking away from the integrity of the treatment. For instance the clinician may say to his client, "I sense that there is part of you that would like if I took total control of your care. This is not possible for me. However, I think we should think together of other sources of support we can get for you."

NEM—managing chronic illness: Chronic illness is likely to be a factor in working with older adults, given that 80 percent of them suffer from it, resulting in physical, emotional, or psychological consequences. There are a number of important interventions and steps that clinicians can take to assist clients with chronic illness management:

1. **Educate yourself:** Clinicians don't have to be knowledgeable about all medical issues, but they do have to research their patients' medical issues and learn the basics about disease management, medications, and their side effects.

2. **Collaborate**: It is highly effective for clinicians to col-

laborate with other medical providers who are treating their older clients, such as primary care providers, nurses, and home care aides. This is in order to closely understand the client's limitations and abilities, and to be able to serve as a support network in clients' overall health and wellbeing. For instance, it may be beneficial to help clients diagnosed with diabetes find the appropriate resources to help them monitor their sugar and comply with their diets. Managing a chronic condition can be demanding and challenging psychologically, emotionally, and physically. As such, I often support my clients in finding ways to organize their schedules so they incorporate exercise, diet, medication, and various lifestyle changes. I also try to link them to various supportive services that can provide concrete services (i.e., home services), as well as social and educational services for their chronic illnesses. I am by no means striving to be a substitute for trained qualified health professionals in the treatment of diabetes; I just want to ensure that clients receive the guidance and support needed to stay on track with their biopsychosocial health.

3. **Cognitive distortions**: As mentioned earlier, another important aspect of assisting older clients with chronic illness is to help them manage psychological reactions to their illness, and in particular the cognitive distortions that can arise. Cognitive distortions are a person's faulty thinking about a certain situation that creates emotional pain and distress. Examples of these include:

(a) *Catastrophizing*, where the patient assumes the worst possible outcome from a medical condition ("This diabetes will kill me"). (b) *Magnifying* has a person inflating a concern ("This diabetic diet will change my entire life"). (c) *Black and white thinking* occurs with clients looking at a situation predict extreme outcomes with no middle ground ("Either I am fully compliant with my diet and medications or I should not even try at all"). (d) *Being a victim*, in which the client personalizes a condition ("I can't believe that this happened to me; why me?") (Kennedy & Tanenbaum, 2000).

The most important intervention with all cognitive distortions is to first be aware of their existence and to help clients understand how they contribute to their distress. Secondly, it is helpful for clients to understand different ways that they can cope with their cognitive distortions. For instance, when clients catastrophize or magnify, they can learn to slow their thought patterns, stay present, and think of other, more-likely outcomes—and know that even with the worst possible outcome, they can cope. Similarly, when clients harbor black or white outcomes, they can again learn to slow thought processes down, think of a middle ground, and be more flexible and kind to themselves by, for instance, saying, "I am doing the best that I can, and that's good for now." With victim distortions, it is important for clients to remind themselves that pain, hurt, and suffering happens to all of us and that it is a part of life. Pain is part of being human, and thinking of ourselves as victims leaves us feeling powerless and hopeless. What we do have control over in regard to pain is how we choose to cope. We can try to view the pain as a learning opportunity, a life lesson, a challenge, and a way to grow, by saying for example, "My medical condition has helped me clarify what I really value in life."

4. **Develop sensorimotor and psychological aware-ness**: The field of psychosomatic medicine has enriched and illuminated our understanding of how unconscious emotions and thoughts can create and/or exacerbate chronic medical conditions. According to the psycho-somatic model, the mind can create actual physical symptoms or aggravate existing disorders such as tension headaches, various back pains, and gastrointestinal issues. These symptoms can divert attention from painful underlying emotional and psychological issues that need to be addressed (Sarno, 2006). I believe that sensorimotor psychotherapy, which is designed to raise somatic and psychological awareness, has an important role in managing chronic illness by helping somatically preoccupied clients focused on physical symptoms to shift their attention to their inner world of emotions, thoughts and memories. It is a way in which clients can learn to stop and identify painful emotions and how they manifest themselves in physical sensations.

Once painful emotions, thoughts, memories, and experiences can be named, verbalized, and accepted, they can take less of a physical toll on us. I have frequently had clients arrive at therapy with severe back pain and migraines, only to report that their symptoms have greatly improved after reaching a level of emotional and psycho-logical awareness and acceptance. A key aspect in helping clients who are somatically preoccupied is to become more mindful of their *core organizers*. The core organizers are defined as the building blocks of our experience, and are comprised of our *thoughts* ("the world is scary"); *emotions* (fear, anger, joy); *five-sense perception* (smell, taste, sight, touch, and hearing); *movement* (from small micro movements to such major motor movements as gestures and facial expressions); and *inner body sensations* (such as feeling hot, weak, energized).

As mentioned earlier, a key component in helping somatically focused clients become more aware is to use mindfulness to enhance awareness of core organizers. Mindfulness has two main components: First, moment-to-moment awareness of what is happening to the client in the here and now within their core organizers. For instance, when discussing their fear, ask how they notice it in their bodies. Secondly, mindfulness requires curiosity and openness to one's experience without attempting to alter or change it. The mind is being trained to observe. To help clients link their bodies to their minds I ask them a key question: "If your pain could express a thought and/or feeling, what would it say? Or, as you discuss this issue, what do you feel inside your body?" A key component of the sensorimotor approach is to help clients interpret their bodily pain as is without adding any value judgement to and learning how to become less reactive to and activated by the physical sensation. Another important aspect of sensorimotor therapy is helping clients develop coping tools known as *resourcing* to manage their discomfort and help ground in their experience of themselves in the current reality in safe and empowered ways. A resource can be a movement, statement, and/or image a client can hold onto when experiencing a certain physical and emotional discomfort (Ogden, 2012).

Nathan, who is a 65-year-old and five years into his second marriage, offers a good example in the use of mindfulness and core organizers. Nathan arrived at therapy after experiencing severe migraines, describing their "hot and powerful flashes of energy." I asked Nathan what the hot flashes say or if they have an emotional feeling to them. After a pause, he replied, "They are saying, 'Not again, not another failed relationship.'" Nathan learned through experimentation in sessions some important resourcing skills to address his hot flashes of pain. These included lengthening his spine, taking deep breaths, and calming himself by saying, "I am doing my best." Once Nathan was able to identify, acknowledge and accept his marital dissatisfaction and process his feelings of hurt, anger, and fear, his symptoms greatly subsided in their frequency and intensity. He was then able to put in place a plan to begin couples therapy, an option he had not considered before.

5. **Behavioral activation**: Clients experiencing chronic illness often feel helpless when it comes to changing such things as destructive lifestyle habits. To address patterns of behavior, it is important to focus on small behavioral changes. In a sense, we are looking for "small wins." For instance, clients seeking to exercise more can start with a daily five-minute walk in the hallway rather than going to the gym.

6. **Chain behavioral analysis**: Chronic illness can be triggered and/or aggravated by certain behaviors. To identify these triggers and behaviors, it is helpful to conduct a chain behavioral analysis. Sometimes a simple shift or change in the client's routine can make a world of difference. A chain behavioral analysis can be accomplished by following the actions of clients step by step before and after their symptoms have been experienced. For example, a chain behavioral analy-

sis for a client who was experiencing gastrointestinal discomfort revealed that it was significantly worse on Mondays, the day a certain home health aide (HHA) would visit. The client disliked the HHA, describing her as "rude and angry." So the HHA was replaced, and the gastrointestinal issues were significantly reduced. If I hadn't conducted a behavior chain analysis, we wouldn't have discovered the connection between the client's dislike for his HHA and the gastrointestinal discomfort, and it may have continued indefinitely.

NEM—loss: As our life progresses, loss may take on many forms, including physical decline, the loss of social and occupational status, the passing of friends and family, and the recognition of the inevitability of our own mortality.

These are all a natural part of aging. It is important for the clinician to feel comfortable discussing issues regarding loss, and view it as an opportunity for client growth. The following areas of intervention can be helpful to focus on when processing any loss:

Naming emotions: When addressing any form of loss, it is important to focus on the ability to process the emotions associated with that loss. With older adults the feelings and thoughts spurred by loss can stay dormant and unprocessed for many years. Supporting older clients in identifying and processing loss may be challenging for clinicians, who may be misled by the elapsed time into thinking that the issues have already been resolved. For example, Dana, a 75-year-old female, only recently began to process her father's suicide, even though she experienced it when she was just nine years old. The event spurred fears of abandonment and greatly impacted her relationships throughout her life.

Simply being able to name the emotions associated with the loss can shed light on it, provide clarity, and serve as a cathartic experience that ultimately can enable the client to accept the painful realization of the loss. It is important not to assume what emotions clients might feel, but rather to allow them to verbalize feelings as they arise. Clients may experience guilt, shame, anger, sadness, relief, and any combination of the above.

Designing a new life: It is important to help clients view loss as part of a transition toward designing a new state of being and life. With the loss of a life partner, clients are challenged to think of other areas of life and opportunities that now may be open to them. If it is a loss of vocational status, clients can be encouraged to identify ways to use their leisure time for spiritual and creative growth. Physical illness and fear of death can bring a sense of awareness to the urgency of time and the need for more meaningful actions and activities. Loss can bring about impetus for positive and meaningful change and putting the loss in perspective can help clients find new meaning and hope. For example I have treated many people who after losing a spouse to a severe, chronic, and debilitating disease, experienced a sense of loss and emptiness combined with a feeling of hope and relief for a better future where they could focus on their own needs and areas for growth.

NEM: Life review is another established intervention I find helpful with older adults. Essentially in psychotherapy all clients conduct some form of life review. However, with older adults, a life review has a highly important and unique significance, as the understanding of the totality of their story is being formulated and judged. The goal of a life review is the formation of an adaptive self-concept about who we are, who we have been, and who we want to become while also gaining a deeper awareness about the story of our lives (Harper & Myers, 2004). The life review intervention, as used by the NEM model, utilizes postmodern psychological theory. Accordingly, postmodern psychology holds that there is no single unified theory that can explain human nature and its ensuing motivations, and likewise there is no one standard that a person can base or judge their behaviors against (Bogdan, 2008). Human nature is complex and multifaceted and there are many different ways to understand and view it. Additionally, according to postmodern psychology much of the knowledge that humans have about themselves is socially constructed; their judgment of their life decisions is formed through a narrow, socially constructed lens of how one "should have" acted according to a socially constructed or rigid and harsh inner standard. The life review method borrows postmodern psychology's emphasis on helping the client view reality from different dimensions and possibilities. This provide clients with an opportunity to rewrite their narrative through a different, more adaptive, and kinder lens.

Life review can be effective when clients express regret, guilt, and a sense of inadequacy, and/or when they want to address certain maladaptive patterns in their lives. A life review can also help clients review a life success and internalize their accomplishments. A major objective of life review is to create a kinder understanding of life decisions. Oftentimes older adults look back at their lives with a sense of regret, self-judgment, and despair. It is important to try and help clients see that the decisions that were made, though not perfect, may have been the only recourse at that phase of their lives and their state at the time. It is important to look at certain events and decisions that clients struggle with and acknowledge the learning experiences and growth that came out of those events. Many painful circumstances and difficult situations in our lives have served as catalysts for positive change.

For example, Jeff, an 80-year-old retired professor, expressed guilt in session for not being more present and available for his son, who is now 50, divorced, and working in a mid-level management position that dissatisfies him.

Jeff expressed how he wished he had provided more guidance, structure, and emotional support to his son which may have helped him to feel "happier" and "more successful" in life. In session, Jeff was able to reach a kinder understanding of his circumstances and acknowledge that, though he was not perfect, he did the best he could under circumstances that found him being a sole breadwinner while also caring for his sick late wife.

To a certain extent our self-concept is shaped by social roles and expectations. Oftentimes older adults look back on their lives and attach certain standards, expectations, and social role norms and judge themselves in an unforgiving way for not meeting those social standards and expectations. Again, the goal here is to help older adults look back at their past behaviors and circumstances in a way that takes into account their unique circumstances and what they were coping with personally. As with the example cited above, a client who believes he was not a good father because he was working too much may be encouraged to acknowledge that during that time he was required to provide for the financial security of his family, which was a priority, and that certain compromises needed to be made.

A life review can also help with exploring and managing an inaccurate and outdated concept of oneself that can lead to anxiety and distress. At times, a client may be attached to a certain role or perception of self that is no longer helpful and that may cause distress. For example, a client with a significant and extensive history of providing caregiving toward family and friends, who is the person everybody turns to for help, may be challenged to become aware of how this role has negatively impacted himself/herself; such people need to learn how to place their needs first and to set limits with those of others.

Again, a life review can be effective when clients express regret, guilt, and a sense of inadequacy and/or when there is the need to address a certain maladaptive pattern that they are struggling with in the here and now.

During the life review process the clinician will assume the role of "editor in chief" and focus on what she/he feels is relevant in accordance to the therapeutic aim of the review. The challenge of conducting a life review is that it can lead down many life paths. As such, it is important to stay focused on the goal that the clinician is trying to address. Use of pictures, letters, journals, and anything that can connect the client in an experiential way to the theme, time, and event under discussion can be powerful.

Life reviews can be done in a variety of ways, and there is no one-size-fits-all standard approach. Many therapists with whom I have worked have creative ways of approaching the review process. The NEM model has a suggested guideline and structure to facilitate a process that is simple and easy to use.

How to conduct a NEM life review:

1. Identify a triggering experience, such as an issue from the past that the client is conflicted about or struggling with, or conversely an experience that the client is proud of, or wants to cherish.

2. Ask the client's permission to conduct a review, and provide him/her with an explanation of how a life review process can be beneficial.

3. Inquire about the stage of life that is being reviewed, including:

   - Set the stage—ask the client to provide you with contextual information of the triggering experience, such as the time period, where the client was living and working, and what life was like for him/her at the time.

   - Explore how the triggering experience began, and who was involved.

   - Ask the client to bring in memorabilia, such as pictures, letters, drawings, and journal entries. These can help connect the clinician and the client to the latter's mindset during the period of time under discussion.

4. Focus on the learning experience obtained from the triggering experience and how it has impacted the patient's view of him/herself, priorities, and life in gen-

eral. In other words, ask what the client has learned about him/herself through this event. Has it impacted his/her priorities?

Has it resulted in a change in what is meaningful to him/her?

5. Explore the impact of the triggering experiences on the client's relationships. Have relationships shifted and changed due to the triggering experience?

6. Establishing a growth mindset is important:

   Ask the client to identify the lessons learned from the triggering experience, how the client would like to see herself/himself, and what she/he would like to focus on in the future.

7. Life as a learning experience:

   Introduce the idea of life as a learning experience, rather than as an event that someone "needs to get right." Inquire about what the client would like to tell their past self if they could talk to them. Is there anything that the triggering experience, albeit difficult, has contributed to the client's life?

8. Develop inner compassion and kindness:

   Challenge clients to develop compassion and kindness for themselves and the lives they have and will continue to be living. Compassion and kindness are skills that can be learned and developed sometimes by just simply observing the ways one is harsh with oneself. Ask clients what they would tell a person in a similar situation and whether they would treat anyone else the same way they are treating themselves. The next segment, which addresses positive aging, also discusses the importance of compassion and kindness.

9. Establishing closure is the final step. Here we explore whether the life review process has changed the way the client experiences him/herself in the here and now. Ask if the review process was helpful and why. And then follow up to see if there are other triggering experiences to be explored.

NEM—positive aging: The final element of the nurturing model is "positive aging," which is defined as "the process of maintaining a positive attitude, feeling good about yourself, keeping fit and healthy, and engaging fully in life as you age" (Hill, 2008).

Utilizing elements from the positive psychology strengths-based approach, positive aging focuses on enhancing strengths rather than managing deficits. It puts an emphasis on growth and the pursuit of opportunities.

Positive aging covers the following principles (Hill, 2008; Halaweh, Ivanoff & Willen, 2018):

Kindness and forgiveness: Far from being a feel-good gesture, the practice of kindness and forgiveness is vital for our wellbeing. Many studies have concluded that showing such compassion to ourselves and to others benefits our mental and physical health and makes us more resilient in the face of adversity. It is vital that we help clients learn to recognize how, and in what ways, they are being harsh and critical with themselves. This harshness, self-judgment and self-criticism may surface so automatically that clients may not realize when it is occurring. Once clients become aware of their self-judgment, we can help them learn how to forgive themselves and view their lives as learning experiences, encouraging them to say to themselves, "We did the best we could." It is then helpful to teach clients to show kindness to themselves, encouraging them simply to talk to themselves as they would to any vulnerable stranger or child. Kindness cannot thrive without forgiveness and forgiveness cannot thrive without kindness. Once clients have learned how to be kind and forgiving to themselves, they can extend it to others, and thus significantly enhance their wellbeing.

This was demonstrated by David, a 72-year-old accountant who had struggled with significant interpersonal problems throughout most of his life. He had never married or engaged in a long-term relationship. David came to therapy feeling very lonely and sad and showing great difficulty in understanding why he struggled with interpersonal relationships. In therapy, we were able to identify a pattern of David being very critical, judgmental, and short with other people, which was driving people away. David had always valued intellect and knowledge and believed that "people are just ignorant." In learning more about David we discovered that he was raised by critical parents who did not reward or praise him for anything but intellectual achievement. As a result, he had adopted a critical, demanding and harsh stance toward himself, feeling that "I am just not smart enough." In therapy David learned to become aware of his self-criticism, and through the practice of self-talk and mindfulness learned to be kind and forgiving toward himself. David said this enabled him to experience a "softening" toward himself and other people. He described being less reactive, more open, and less angry. He has fostered new relationships through his synagogue and has more conversations with his neighbors. Though still not perfect, David learned to nurture a very different relationship with his critical self.

Finding meaning and purpose: Finding meaning is vital for positive aging. Meaning and purpose are the driving forces in our lives. Every life on Earth has meaning and purpose. Sometimes due to adverse life experiences, trauma, loss, illness, and abuse, clients may feel that they have lost meaning, or feel disconnected from it. Helping clients connect to whatever it is that provides their lives with meaning and purpose is important. With older clients, finding meaning applies not only to the present and future, but also to the past. It is important to help older adult clients infuse the narrative of their lives with meaning and purpose. Older clients who struggle with regrets and missed opportunities can be helped by exploring with them how their struggles and losses have been part of a bigger narrative that perhaps provided their lives with greater meaning and purpose.

One example of this was provided by an older client of mine. While reflecting on the agony of losing his daughter to a prolonged terminal illness, he related how, through his daughter's illness, he gained an appreciation of what he valued and what mattered to him. He began slowing down, accepting the fleetingness of life, appreciating the here and now and time well-spent with family and friends.

Creative and intellectual stimulation: Another important element in positive aging is an emphasis on continued learning and creative stimulation. Numerous studies have confirmed the significant impact that continued intellectual growth has on overall psychological and physical wellbeing. As such, encouraging clients to be active learners is vital. I often strongly urge clients to engage in such recreational pursuits as music, painting, yoga, and book clubs. I also encourage them to return to hobbies and interests that they pursued in the past and dropped. I remember the joy of one client who returned to his photography hobby after a lapse of several years and rediscovered his creative self.

I find it helpful to conduct a hobby and leisure inventory by asking clients what interests they currently have, or had in the past. This can help them develop awareness, motivation, and a plan to re-engage in creative and learning activities.

Attitude of gratitude: We instinctively focus on what we are missing, lacking, and on what pains and afflicts us. Redirecting our awareness to what we have and what we are grateful for is less habitual and can require mental effort. However, research has shown that once we develop an attitude of gratitude through consistent practice, it can improve our mental health. For example, a study by Neall Krause (2017) shows an association between gratitude and a reduced amount of the protein A1, which is associated with heart disease. I often encourage my clients to name two things they are grateful for each morning. This can set a positive tone for the day and also develops gratitude muscles.

Strengthening social relationships: Strengthening our relationships is vital for our mental and physical wellbeing. Research has shown that older adults who have positive interpersonal relationships report feeling happier, and are at reduced risk for developing dementia and heart disease (Burr, Han & Taveras, 2015). In another study (Sneed & Cohen, 2014), it was argued that the risk of social isolation is comparable to that of drinking and smoking. As such, improving and sustaining our interpersonal relationships is not just an issue of comfort and lifestyle, it is a major health factor that needs to be addressed. I encourage all my clients to reach out to their support networks and participate in social activities with local community and/or religious organizations. There is a misconception that older adults are unable or unwilling to use technology. However current research shows that about two-thirds of those sixty-five and older are online and four of every ten seniors own a smartphone. Current technologies can provide older adults with an array of needed services, such as telemedicine (ability to receive clinical medical services online with a provider); access to health information; connection with friends and family; participation in online classes; and access to transportation applications such as Lyft and Uber. New technologies are also being developed to monitor the health and care of older adults.

Today, with social media, clients can feel connected in ways they never could before. For example a home monitoring system used by clients at Weill Cornell Medicine's Center on Aging and Behavioral Research alerts family members through emails and texts if clients have not eaten or taken their medications by a certain time of the day. Gerontologist Sara Czaja, PhD, and her associates have developed the Personal Reminder Information and Social Management (PRISM) system. This was designed with the input of seniors to make it user-friendly and suitable for the physical and cognitive needs of older adults. It includes streamlined access to emails, links to various resources, video games, and a calendar. It has easy-to-read fonts and a "buddy tab" that allows the user to connect to others with similar interests with the click of a button. A study showed that older adults using PRISM for a period of one year reported feeling significantly less lonely and scored higher on wellbeing than those who didn't use it (Selarno, 2019).

The technology revolution is providing significant opportunities for older adults to enhance their wellbeing. It is vital that we as clinicians empower, educate, and support them in utilizing these invaluable resources.

Now let's read a Nurturing Environment Model case example to show you NEM in practice.

Meet Jacob, 74 years old.

The initial referral came from a relative who was concerned about Jacob's anxiety, anger, and compulsive calling of family members who were overwhelmed by managing and supporting him with his fears of aging, loneliness, loss, and regret. Jacob lived alone and didn't have children. His ex-wife, who was 25 years younger, had divorced him three years previously for "another man," as Jacob put it. Concurrently with the separation from his wife, Jacob's brother, with whom he was close, passed away. These two calamities were traumatic for Jacob, making him dependent on his extended family. Jacob, a retired lawyer, had stopped painting, playing the piano, and reading—hobbies he once loved.

His nephew reported that Jacob would call several times a day, and would complain of feeling "abandoned" if phone calls were not returned within minutes. Jacob was diagnosed with diabetes and struggled with weakness in his legs which resulted in periodic falls, especially in the middle of the night. Jacob described feeling hopeless about his diabetes and changing his diet, which often consisted of pasta and bread.

Initially, Jacob was reluctant to receive help from a therapist and viewed me as an outsider; he struggled with trusting others. A look into Jacob's childhood can help explain some of his trust issues. His mother had been extremely physically and emotionally abusive to him and his father had been passive and offered little protection and guidance. He would often describe how his mother would hit, blame, and curse him for no apparent reason. As a result, Jacob learned to distrust his feelings and would immediately cut off anybody with whom he felt uncomfortable. This was a pattern that could be seen in the many friendships he ended over the years.

When meeting with Jacob, he said he'd like to work on "not feeling lonely" and to understand why people in his life "abandoned" him. He discussed his regret for being in a relationship with a woman who betrayed him. He also related how he lacked meaning in his life and asked often, "What do I have to live for?"—though he always denied having suicidal ideations. Jacob also discussed wanting help with the intense anxiety and panic attacks he experienced throughout the day.

We began our work.

In looking at the transference, at times it felt that Jacob viewed me as a parent whom he couldn't trust, yet felt dependent upon. He also viewed me as an authority figure and at times, would also view me as the "son I never had," with the implicit expectation that I care for him as if he were my father. I felt from Jacob a mixture of dependence and, at the same time, distrust, which was often expressed as a fear that "you will leave me like all the rest." I, in turn, had a strong parental countertransference toward Jacob and at times was aware of the responsibility I was feeling for him, as though he were my elder father. But I was also very much aware of my need for distance and space, and at times felt his fear and dependence to be engulfing and consuming.

In sessions with Jacob, I did utilize his transference toward me to try and foster awareness of his need for attachment and feelings of vulnerability. For example, I would typically ask Jacob how he felt about me and our relationship, and he would often respond, "I hope you're not going to leave me and that I am not disappointing you." These honest feelings about our relationship would open a wonderful door to exploring other past and current relationships in Jacob's life and how those fears of abandonment played out and impacted his relationships.

In one session Jacob was able to say, "You must be overwhelmed by me." I asked him how he felt he was being overwhelming, and he was able to own that at times he experienced himself as demanding and angry and that this may "drive people away."

This acknowledgment by Jacob resulted in a growing empathy for his relatives. He was able to change his way of communicating his fear by being less demanding, and he also began taking an interest in different aspects of his cousins' lives. Jacob was able to acknowledge that "I don't want to overwhelm the people I need the most." Developing awareness of his transference reactions toward me allowed Jacob to manage his other relationships better. In turn, managing my own countertransference in taking care of Jacob through supervision allowed me to be less reactive to my need to treat him as if I were a loyal son, and set better limits and focus on reaching our therapeutic goals.

In assisting Jacob in managing his chronic medical conditions, I encouraged him to begin meeting regularly with a primary care provider—something he did not have at the time of our initial appointment. Once this was in place, I collaborated with the provider regularly to ensure that Jacob had follow-up appointments, and discussed his progress. Assisting Jacob in changing his lifestyle, including diet and exercise, was vital for his health. I reminded Jacob to fill out his diabetes log and monitor his sugar level. Helping Jacob express and manage his thoughts and feelings around his health was an effective path to making them less overwhelming. Jacob was very somatically preoccupied and often discussed his overall physical pain and discomfort. I tried to help him develop awareness of how he holds his emotions in his body. When Jacob discussed instances where he felt sad, afraid, and abandoned, I would ask him how he would experience these feelings in his body, which he described—after a long pause— "like being torn from the inside." I asked Jacob to stay with the feeling of being torn from the inside and helped him develop resources to cope with those sensations, such as deep breathing, engaging in a calming pacing movement, and telling himself such things as "be kind to myself."

Educating Jacob on his negative thoughts, in particular his "catastrophizing," was helpful in gaining better control over them. Through a chain behavioral analysis, I determined that most of Jacob's falls occurred when he awoke to go to the bathroom in the middle of the night when he was feeling drowsy. I discussed with Jacob and his physician the possibility of wearing adult diapers at night, which he agreed to, and these significantly reduced his falling episodes.

Managing Jacob's losses comprised a major part of our work together, enabling him to process his deprivation of a secure childhood. He was able to connect to the pain of the "little Jacob" so many years ago, and understand how the trauma of his childhood was impacting him to this very day. During our sessions he said, "I guess there is a scared little Jacob I take with me wherever I go." Jacob was able to connect and process the death of his brother and express feelings of sadness, anger, guilt, and shame in ways he had never been able to before. For instance, he was able to verbalize feelings of anger he felt toward his brother because his death had triggered feelings of abandonment. He was also able to express his guilt over having such feelings toward his brother, who he loved. Finally, Jacob was able to process the separation from his wife and grieve the loss of this relationship. He was able to both accept his anger and longing for his former wife: "I loved her very much, but she hurt me deeply as well, and there is not a day that goes by without thinking of her." Jacob was able to reflect on how he grew in this relationship and integrated both the loss and the joy of the relationship, and thus he was able to transform feelings of resentment to acceptance and gratitude. Jacob was able to express the loss of his youth, decline of his health, and his fear of aging: "It scares me that I will die alone and helpless." We were able to focus on the importance of staying in the here and now, and concentrate on the abilities and the experiences he can still have while simultaneously validating his fears and loss.

In reflecting and processing the many losses he had experienced, Jacob was able to gain a new perspective on each one of them. Jacob was able to connect to his sense of strength and resilience, and develop hope for the future by being more fully present in the here and now. The focus of the life review we conducted had involved Jacob's belief that his life was a "failure," leaving him feeling alone, sad, and empty. I felt that Jacob was narrowing his life to one, very painful, defining word and asked that we conduct a life review to evaluate this. I suggested that he bring to our session pictures of his childhood, girlfriends, college certificate, as well as photographs of his business and travel experiences. I was trying to help Jacob connect to the many positive experiences of his past by going back in time and trying to relive them through the life review. For instance, he was able to reflect on the positive response of a customer who had said, "This is the best customer service I have ever received." Jacob was able to connect to the academic, creative, and romantic experiences he had had with various partners. And he was also able to recollect his many adventures and experiences such as living in a recreational vehicle for a year. All of this allowed him to acknowledge that his life had been special and unique, and that "many people would have paid anything to have had these experiences." Conducting a life review for the purpose of connecting to his achievements was very beneficial, allowing Jacob to see that his notion of being a failure was a fleeting thought with no significant substance.

Positive aging was a significant element of the work with Jacob. I frequently infused into our sessions the importance that he be more "kind to himself." Noticing how harsh and critical he had been to himself in the past, the first step was to help him develop a stance of compassion. I asked that he allow himself the same respect he would show to anyone else. We all have experiences and events that we can either perceive as failures or learning experiences. I asked that Jacob view his apparent failures as events that enhanced his awareness of what he wanted for himself; in the case of his wife divorcing him, for instance, he observed, "I suddenly understood how lonely I really am and have always been."

We were able to connect to where Jacob derives his meaning and purpose, enabling him to learn that people and connections "is what I value the most." We devised a plan of how and where he could meet people for instance, by developing a Facebook account and by attending a local senior center. I remember going with Jacob to meet with the director of the senior center because at first he felt anxious about going alone. We discussed the possibility that he play the piano and return to making pottery. I looked up classes in pottery and computer design that Jacob could join. During holidays, when Jacob was afraid of being alone, I looked up local church activities he could participate in. I helped him utilize his intellectual curiosity by discussing various interesting articles he had read, or by discussing his political opinions. I noticed that these discussions gave him vitality and a place to organize his thoughts and emotions on issues he was passionate about. I encouraged Jacob to reconnect with old friends with whom he had lost contact. I got him to purchase and set up a computer system so he could use online resources and connect to social media. Because purchasing a computer and learning to use it was initially daunting to Jacob, I enlisted the support of a tech-savvy family member to visit him at home and guide him. Jacob today greatly enjoys online activities and connecting through social media. I also asked Jacob to practice gratitude, and each day upon waking and before going to sleep reflect on two or three things he is grateful for. All these positive aging activities have significantly enriched Jacob's life and activity level.

I would like to end my case example regarding Jacob with a Zen proverb: A Japanese Zen master named Nan-in (1868–1912) received a university professor who inquired about Zen. Nan-in poured tea into his visitor's cup until it overflowed, and kept pouring. Said the professor, not able to restrain himself, "It is overflowing; no more will go in." Nan-in responded: "Like this cup, you are full of your wrong opinions and speculations. How can I show you Zen unless you first empty your cup?" As much as I impacted Jacob, he reshaped and transformed me. Like the proverb of Nan-in, working with Jacob has allowed me the precious opportunity to empty my cup of preconceived biases and assumptions regarding work with older adults. It has taught me how important, transformative, and meaningful our work with older adults can be. We are always in the process of becoming and growing. Older age can provide us with a unique opportunity to achieve a level of psychological, emotional, and spiritual growth not seen in any other age. It is up to us, the clinicians, to provide a nurturing environment for this growth to happen.

DEMENTIA

It is important for anyone working with older adults to know the basics on assessing for and behaviorally managing dementia.

Between 35 percent and 50 percent of people over age 85 years have dementia. Most clients with dementia do not necessarily present with a complaint of memory loss; it is often a spouse, other family member, or friend who brings the problem to the clinician's attention. Symptoms of dementia can include one or more of the following:

- Difficulty in retaining new information—for example, trouble remembering events, dates, and numbers.

- Difficulty in handling complex tasks like balancing a checkbook.

- Difficulty with reasoning—being unable to cope with unexpected events and think through new and demanding situations, for instance.

- Difficulty with spatial ability and orientation—getting lost in familiar places, perhaps.

- Difficulty with language, like not knowing how to say a word.

- Behavior that seems unorganized and bizarre, such

as walking in a certain direction without purpose, and not knowing why.

It is important to note that we all have memory lapses or periods when we feel disorganized, especially in times of stress or fatigue. But what we see in clients diagnosed with dementia is consistency, chronicity, and continued deterioration across the board in all areas of their lives.

Dementia is a progressive disease that is often preceded by a stage of mild cognitive impairment (MCI). This is generally defined by the presence of memory difficulties, but preserved ability to function in daily life. The key difference between MCI and dementia is that with the latter a person can lose the ability to function independently and perform daily tasks. As such, MCI could be considered an intermediate stage between normal aging and dementia.

The normal cognitive decline associated with aging is manifested by diminished ability to learn new information, but no loss in memory retention. Memory problems come with MCI, and the loss of functioning is associated with dementia.

It is important to look at cognitive function decline in older adults as a continuum, with the first level involving the normal process of aging characterized mainly by a diminished ability to learn new tasks. This is followed by MCI, involving some memory difficulty but a retained ability to function independently. Then comes dementia, involving memory decline and an inability to function, or at least a progressive inability to function independently.

Before concluding that a client has dementia, it is important to conduct an assessment of the following issues:

- Review the client's drug history and determine whether she/he is using drugs that impair cognition and create the impression of dementia, such as analgesics, anticholinergics, psychotropic medications, and sedative-hypnotics.

- Consumption of illicit substances such as cocaine and the use of alcohol should also be assessed for. It is important to note that drugs can be used and abused at any age. For instance, a study showed that nearly 50 percent of nursing home residents have alcohol-related problems.

- Structural neuroimaging with head CT or MRI scans can be considered in the initial evaluation of all clients with dementia to identify structural damage to the brain.

- Screening for B12 deficiency and hypothyroidism is recommended for clients being evaluated for dementia.

- Screening for depression in clients with dementia is recommended because it is a common treatable comorbidity that can masquerade as dementia. Clients who are depressed typically report difficulty remembering and feeling confused, symptoms very common in dementia.

- The Mini-Mental State Exam is a useful, validated, and very common screening test for dementia; a score of less than 24 points is suggestive of dementia or delirium. It is very easy to use and can identify clients who are at risk for dementia.

As I mentioned earlier, it is usually a family member and/or friends who identify a problem and reach out for help. Therefore, it is important to know what questions to ask these informants. The Washington University Dementia Screening Test is a validated instrument that clinicians can utilize (listed in the reference). Some of the symptoms and changes associated with dementia include the following:

- Problems with judgment where, suddenly, simple problem-solving tasks are not possible. Getting lost, but not thinking of asking for help from a passer-by

- Reduced interest in hobbies/activities

- Repetition of questions, stories, or statements

- Trouble learning how to use a tool or appliance

- Forgetting the correct month or year

- Difficulty handling financial affairs, such as bill-paying and taxes, which become overwhelming and undoable

- Difficulty remembering appointments

- Consistent problems with thinking and/or memory

Neuropsychiatric symptoms are common in dementia. These may impact client's mood, thoughts, and behavioral patterns. Such symptoms can include agitation, aggression, delusions, hallucinations, wandering, depression, apathy, disinhibition, and sleep disturbances. These symptoms can create great distress, both for clients and caregivers (Alexander & Press, 2018).

Behavioral interventions for dementia: When working with older adults with dementia, it is vital to know important behavioral interventions that can effectively manage their symptoms.

Neuropsychiatric symptoms associated with dementia, such as aggression and agitation, can be triggered by environmental stressors. As such, it is helpful to conduct chain behavioral analysis of any preceding events that generate agitation, and to determine whether these stressful triggers can be anticipated, modified, avoided, and alleviated. Reducing and avoiding environmental triggers can help reduce and/or eliminate stressful reactions.

Clients in even the most advanced stages of dementia can still relate to the world through their senses. As such, any intervention that is soothing to the senses can be effective. For example, a client who is highly agitated during visiting hours may benefit from having fewer visitors at once in order to reduce the level of sensory excitement (Bird & Blair, 2010).

There are some evidence-based holistic therapies that utilize patients' senses that have been proven to be effective. These include:

- Aromatherapy involving such scents as lemon balm or lavender oil is frequently used, and can be delivered either through inhalation or skin application

- Exercise training in combination with caregiver education may improve outcomes in clients with Alzheimer's disease (AD)

- Music therapy

- Pet therapy

- Massage and touch therapy appear to be potentially beneficial in the immediate management of agitated behavior

- In addition to the above, caregivers can be counseled in strategies involving distraction and redirection, structured routines, and calming reassuring responses for clients who seem anxious

It is also important to become somewhat familiar with the various names of medications used to treat dementia and their side effects. Dementia entails dead brain cells and weakened/lost connections between cells. Though currently there is no medication that can cure dementia, there are treatments geared toward slowing its progression.

Most medications approved by the FDA to treat early-to-moderate dementia symptoms are from a class of drugs called cholinesterase inhibitors. These work by increasing a chemical in the brain called acetylcholine that aids in memory and judgment. The medications include:

- Donepezil (Aricept)

- Galantamine (Razadyne)

- Rivastigmine (Exelon)

The more common side effects of cholinesterase inhibitors include nausea, vomiting, diarrhea, and dizziness.

Among another class of medications used to treat moderate-to-severe dementia is memantine, a drug that functions by increasing the chemical glutamate which can help in improving information processing. The drugs most commonly used in this class are Namenda and Namzaric. The side effects most associated with the aforementioned medications are vomiting, nausea, confusion, dizziness, increased bowel movements, and headaches.

It is important to note that the efficacy of these drugs is still being debated. Some studies exhibit only very short-term benefits (Alexander & Press, 2018).

Finally, I would also like to mention the importance of providing ongoing encouragement, guidance, and assistance to the client support network. Family and friends may need guidance on how to manage dementia clients' reactions, and on how to obtain psychological counseling for themselves due to the tremendous emotional burden that they face on a daily basis. Caregiver burnout is a well-known problem, and treating the support network is vital for the success of the treatment process. It is important for clinicians treating clients with dementia to be open, ready, and willing to coach, treat, and refer the client support network for support when needed.

IN CLOSING

Older adulthood is a vital stage in human development encompassing important and meaningful challenges, both in terms of the client's past and future. Our perception of people at this stage in life has been shaped by social and cultural influences. In contrast to the negative stigma associated with older people in psychotherapy, this cohort is highly rewarding to work with. Older adults bring with them wisdom, maturity, patience, thoughtfulness, and motivation to the psychotherapeutic process. There is a great call for psychotherapeutic work with older adults, whose needs are at times overlooked and missed as a result of societal biases and their tendency to not seek help. Older adults struggle with various emotional, psychological, trauma, social, and substance abuse issues and the importance in meeting and addressing their needs is real and vital. In order to provide effective care, it is important for clinicians to be aware and informed of the elements of normative aging and be able to differentiate between normal and pathological aging. Older adults tend to bring to psychotherapy unique issues and needs that need to be addressed, and it is vital that clinicians familiarize themselves with the range of social, emotional, and psychological issues with which this group struggles. The therapeutic relationship is the most vital component of the psychotherapeutic process, and it is important for clinicians to familiarize themselves with the various ways they can enhance it. I am hoping that the NEM approach delineated in this handbook will provide clinicians with a helpful model to provide care to older adults. Finally, as more people enter older age, dementia will continue to be a major and prevalent medical condition that clinicians need to be aware of and informed of in terms of assessment and available treatment methods.

I am hoping that this booklet has shed some light on the psychotherapeutic work with this population. Most importantly, I hope that more older adults will ask for help and will choose to engage in the important and meaningful work of psychotherapy. It is also my hope that clinicians will continue to open their minds and hearts to the important work to be done with older people.

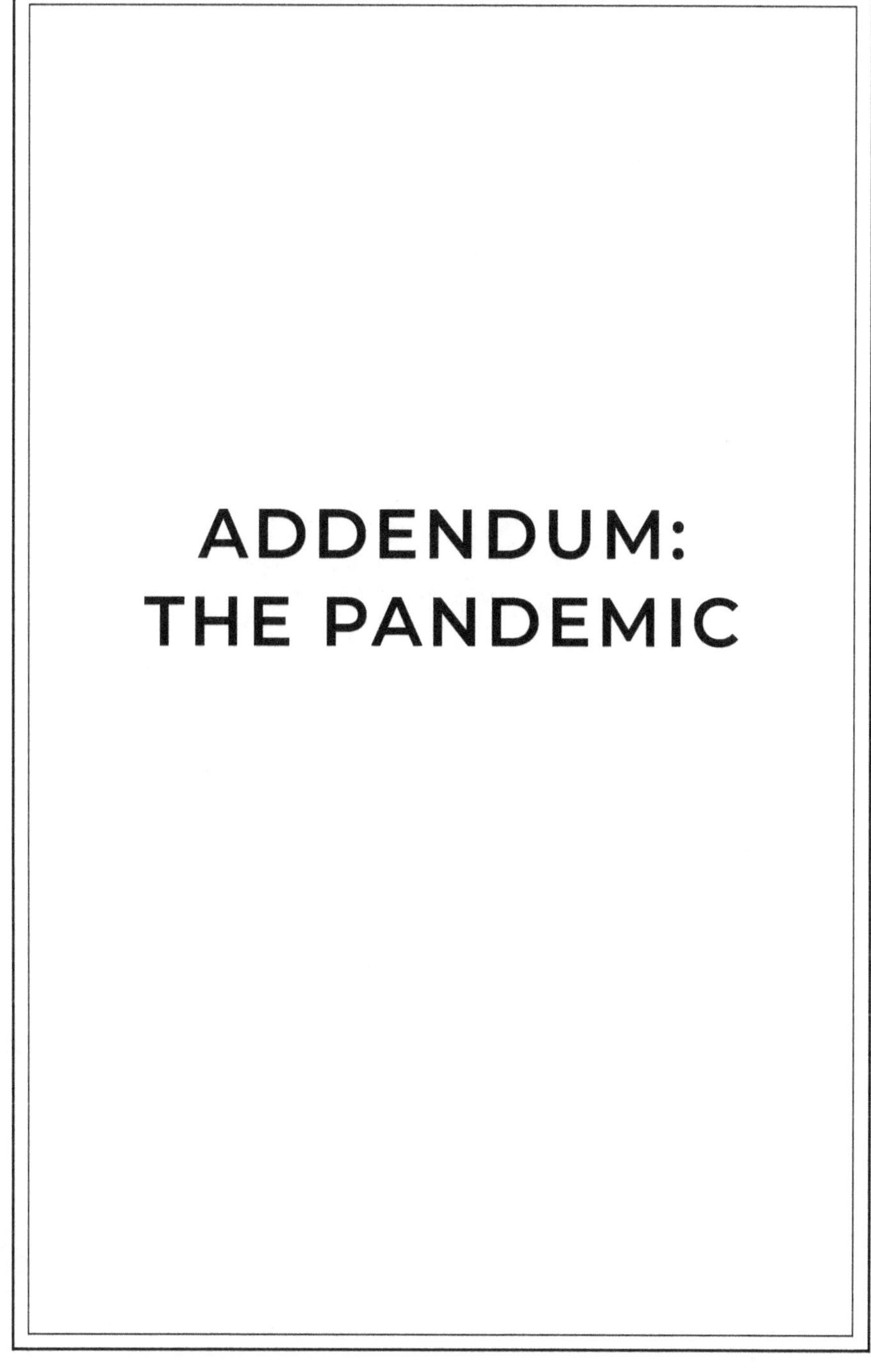

ADDENDUM:
THE PANDEMIC

Towards the conclusion of this book, a major pandemic impacted the world and hit the shores of the U.S. As I write these lines, the COVID-19 virus has thus far infected more than 4.6 million people worldwide and killed more than three hundred thousand. Older adults have been among the most vulnerable victims of this virus. An estimated 8.6% of patients age 70 and above and 13.4% ages 80 and older will die from COVID-19 (Verity et al., 2020) and approximately one third of all COVID-19 deaths in the U.S. have occurred in long-term care nursing homes (Yourish et al., 2020).

The pandemic will impact our older clients in many ways. Here are suggestions and considerations for clinicians working with older adults:

1. The psychotherapist needs now to prepare to step into the role of protective advocate, someone who can educate and guide the client to make safe choices during this time. This may involve educating the client on issues around the use of protective gear (such as face masks), testing, social distancing, maintaining active hygiene, and educating about the use of technological platforms for connections (such as Zoom), all of which has become an integral part of the therapeutic encounter with our clients.

2. The emotional and psychological needs during the COVID-19 have become ever more complex and challenging. Due to the emphasis on maintaining social distancing, older adults, who at their baseline were already vulnerable to loneliness and social isolation, have experienced a heightened feeling of loneliness and isolation. Older adults have been separated from their family in ways which have deprived them the ability to connect, touch, and communicate with their family and community. Clinicians can play a vital role in helping clients feel connected by providing a therapeutic holding environment where clients can experience an emotional connection and their needs for social engagement can be met. Hearing the tone of our voice, feeling understood, and seeing our faces (if using a video platform) can be extremely beneficial in helping our clients regulate their nervous system.

3. The loss of daily routines, structure, and activities which have been an essential part of our clients well-being have been replaced with social isolation, inactivity in confined and closed spaces, and a sedentary lifestyle. The fear of the unknown as to how long the pandemic will last and when life will return to what it was have all highteened our levels of anxiety and fear. Adjusting to this "new reality" has been a challenging part of the work with so many of our clients. Clinicians can play a vital role in assisting clients developing new routines, schedules, and activities. It is vital that our clients establish a new routine as soon as possible. Clinicians can play a vital role in assisting

clients in establishing new routines which are safe and productive.

4. The ongoing worry about COVID-19 infection, illness, and death could result in an ongoing heightened stress response resulting in weaker immune systems, insomnia and possible increased vulnerability to other underlying health conditions such as heart disease, hypertension, and diabetes. Additionally, many clients may forgo their routine medical appointments and/or avoid going to the emergency room if they don't feel well because of fear of possible infection, all of which can pose great risk for the overall health of the client. Clinicians working with older adults can play a vital role in teaching clients stress management and self care skills such as meditation, exercise, sleep hygiene, nutrition, and advocating and encouraging for management of their ongoing relationship with care providers through in person or online appointments is vital.

5. Due to rules about social distancing and hospital safety policies, another very tragic and cruel aspect of this pandemic is that many COVID patients have died alone without the ability to spend the last moments with their loved ones. The fear of dying alone is a very real possibility. Many families have been experiencing this tragic and profound hurt as a result of the inability to care for and be with their loved ones as they pass. Additionally, the ability to hold funerals and grieve normally has been robbed from and disrupted for so many of us. Clinicians working with older adults can

play a vital role in helping older adults process the losses of their friends and loved ones as well as prepare for the possibility of illness and death. Hoping for the best, managing expectations, and planning for the worst, such as writing letters to loved ones now, can be an emotional process but can result in patients feeling less anxious, more secure, and grounded.

6. The psychiatrist and Holocaust survivor Viktor Frankl said that if we are no longer able to change a situation, we are challenged to change ourselves. Through this pandemic I have witnessed great hurt and pain but also moments of true appreciation, joy, and growth. Clients who all of a sudden have had the experience of slowing down, spending time with their families, and evaluating their priorities have been forever transformed. Accompanying our clients on their individual journey to seek meaning and purpose through this pandemic can be a tremendously challenging and rewarding process. As for us, I believe that there has never been a more important and meaningful time to provide support for our older adults. I am hoping that we can all rise to the important calling of being there for our older adults in this very frightening and vulnerable time.

BIBLIOGRAPHY

Alzheimer's Association. (2018) Alzheimer's Disease Facts and Figures. Retrieved from https://www.alz.org/media/HomeOffice/Facts%20 and%20Figures/facts-and-figures.pdf

Bengtson, V. L., & Allen, K. R. (1993). The life course perspective applied to families over time. In P. G. Boss, W. J. Doherty, R. LaRossa, W. R. Schumm, & S. K. Steinmetz (eds.), *Sourcebook of Family Theories and Methods: A Contextual Approach* (pp. 469–504). New York, NY: Plenum Press.

Bird, M., & Blair, A. (2010). "Clinical Psychology and Anxiety and Depression in Dementia: Three Case Studies." *Nordic Psychology*, 62 (2), 43–54.

Bogdan, B. (2008). "Why Does Psychotherapy Need Postmodernism?" *Archives of Psychiatry and Psychotherapy*, 3, 43–50.

Burr, J. A., Han, S. H., & Taveras, M. S. (2015). "Volunteering and Cardiovascular Disease Risk: Does Helping Others Get 'Under the Skin'?" *The Gerontologist*, 56 (1), 937–947.

Ellen, A. (2013). "How Therapy Can Help in the Golden Years." *New York Times*. Retrieved from https://well.blogs.nytimes.com/2013/04/22/ how-therapy-can-help-in-the-golden-years/

Erikson, E. (1951). Childhood and Society, London: Imago.

Frankl, V. (1992). Man's Search for Meaning. Beacon Press: Boston. https://www.thelancet.com/journals/laninf/article/ PIIS1473-3099(20)30243-7/fulltext

Gorsuch, N. (1998). "Time's Winged Chariot: Short-term Psychotherapy in Later Life." *Psychodynamic Counseling*, 4 (2), 191–202.

Harper, M. C, & Myers, J. E. (2004). "Evidenced-Based Practice with Older Adults." *Journal of Counseling and Development*, 82 (2), 207–218.

Hill, R. D (2009). *Seven Strategies for Positive Aging*. New York. W.W. Norton and Company.

Huffington Post. (2014). "Seven Cultures that Celebrate Aging and Respect Their Elders." Retrieved from https://www.huffpost.com/entry/ what-other-cultures-can-teach_n_4834228

Jung, C.G. (1933). *Modern Man in Search of a Soul*, London: Pelican

Kennedy, G. J, & Tanenbaum, S. (2000). "Psychotherapy with Older Adults." *American Journal of Psychotherapy*, Summer 54 (3), 386–395.

King, P. (1974). Notes on Psychoanalysis of Older Patients, *British Journal of Analytical Psychology* 19: 22-37.

Knight, B. G (1996). *Psychotherapy with Older Adults* (2nd ed.). Thousand Oaks, CA: Sage Publications.

Krause, N., Emmons, R. A., Ironson, G., & Hill, P. C. (2017). "General Feelings of Gratitude to God and Hemoglobin A1C: Exploring Variations by Gender." *Journal of Positive Psychology*, 12(6), 639–650.

Lewis, J. L., & Johansen, K. H. (1982). "Resistance to Psychotherapy with the Elderly." *American Journal of Psychotherapy*, 36 (4), 497–504.

National Institute on Aging (April 23, 2019). "Social Isolation, Loneliness in Older People Pose Health Risks." Retrieved from https://www.nia.nih.gov/news/ social-isolation-loneliness-older-people-pose-health-risks

Nordhus, I.H & Nielsen, G.H (1999). Brief Dynamic Psychotherapy with Older Adults. *Clinical Psychology*, 55 (8), 935-947.

Press. D & Alexander M. (2018). Treatment of Dementia. UpToDate. Retrieved from https://www.uptodate.com/contents/ treatment-of-dementia

Ogden, P. (2012). *Sensorimotor Psychotherapy Institute Level I Training Manual: Training in Affect Dysregulation, Survival Defenses and Traumatic Memory.*

Sarno, J.E. (2006). The Divided Mind: *The Epidemic of Mindbody Disorders*. New York. HarperCollins Publishers.

Selarno, H. (2019). Tech Therapy. Magazine of Weill Cornell Medicine, Winter edition, 35-39.

Sneed.R.S., & Cohen.S. (2014). Negative Social Interactions and Incident Hypertension Among Older Adults. *Health Psychology*, June; 33 (6), 554-65.

Sushi, D. (2016). "What Indians can Teach About Aging." Special Broadcasting Services. Retrived from https://www.sbs.com.au/topics/ voices/culture/article/2016/06/09/what-indians-can-teach-us-about-aging

Sutin, A.R (et.al). (2013). The Effect of Birth Cohort on Well-Being: The Legacy of Economic Hard Times. *Psychological Science*, 24(3), 379-385.

Verity, R. (2020). Estimates of the severity of coronavirus disease 2019: a model based analysis. The Lancet Infectious Diseases. Retrieved from https://www.thelancet.com/journals/laninf/article/PIIS1473-3099(20)30243-7/fulltext

Woods, R.T. (1999). Mental health problems in later life. Chichester: Wiley.

World Health Organization on Mental Health of Older Adults. (2017). Retrieved from https://www.who.int/news-room/fact-sheets/detail/mental-health-of-older-adults

Yesavage, J.A, & Karasu, T.B. (1982). Psychotherapy with Elderly Patients. *American Journal of Psychotherapy*, 36(1), 41-55.

Yourish, K., Lai, R., Ivory, D., & Smith.,M. (2020). One-Third of all U.S. Coronavirus Deaths Are Nursing Home Residents or Workers. New York Times. Retrieved from https://www.nytimes.com/interactive/2020/05/09/us/coronavirus-cases-nursing-homes-us.html

APPENDIX-1: ASSESSMENT INSTRUMENTS

Galvin, J.E. (2018). The AD8: The Washington University Dementia Screening Test. Try This, Issue D14. Retrieved from https://consultgeri.org/try-this/dementia/issue-d14.pdf

Greenberg, S. Geriatric Depression Scale (GDS). (2019). Try This, Issue Number 4. Retrieved from https://consultgeri.org/try-this/general-assessment/issue-4.pdf

Naegle, A.N. (2018). Alcohol Use Screening and Assessment for Older Adults. Try This, Issue Number 17. Retrieved from https://consultgeri.org/try-this/general-assessment/issue-17.pdf

Yaffe MJ, Wolfson C, Lithwick M, Weiss D. Development and validation of a tool to improve physician identification of elder abuse: The Elder Abuse Suspicion Index (EASI) ©. Journal of Elder Abuse and Neglect 2008; 20(3) 000-000.com. Retrieved from: https://medicine.uiowa.edu/familymedicine/sites/medicine.uiowa.edu.familymedicine/files/wysiwyg_uploads/EASI.pdf

ABOUT THE AUTHOR

Amir Levine, Ph.D., LCSW-R, is the Co-Founder and Clinical Director of Bhava Therapy Group based in New York City. Bhava Therapy Group provides psychotherapy and continuing education training rooted in the values of compassionate presence and action, respect, accountability, professional integrity, holistic support and humility. For over a decade, Dr. Levine served as the Director of Behavioral Science at the Bronx Lebanon Hospital, Department of Family Medicine where he built the team of behavioral science and mental health clinicians and developed and directed the behavioral medicine training curriculum for medical professionals. Dr. Levine completed his Masters Degree and Ph.D. in Social Work from the Wurzweiler School of Social Work at Yeshiva University.

As the Clinical Director of the Bhava Therapy Group team of therapists, Dr. Levine serves as a devoted mentor, educator, and mental health provider. Dr. Levine has presented at numerous national conferences and directs the Bhava Therapy Group Continuing Education Program where he facilitates workshops on providing psychotherapy for older adults, holistic treatment of personality disorders and on additional topics.

Dr. Levine is deeply passionate about the psychotherapeutic work he is doing with his older adult clients. His therapeutic model is informed by the many clients he has had the honor of working with, viewing these individuals as his best teachers and sources of inspiration.

Born in Israel, Dr. Levine spent time growing up in both Israel and the United States and has been residing in the U.S. for the past 18 years. Having this bicultural exposure has served to expand Dr. Levine's sensibilities to the differences that exist in humanity and his openness to and love of learning about every individual's unique life journey.

Dr. Levine is grateful to live in NY State with his wife, two children and their dog Molly.

www.ingramcontent.com/pod-product-compliance
Lightning Source LLC
Chambersburg PA
CBHW021114130726
47988CB00003B/1012